A
SHORT
HISTORY OF
FINANCIAL
EUPHORIA

ALSO BY JOHN KENNETH GALBRAITH

AMERICAN CAPITALISM:
THE CONCEPT OF COUNTERVAILING POWER

A THEORY OF PRICE CONTROL

ECONOMICS AND THE ART OF CONTROVERSY

THE GREAT CRASH, 1929

THE AFFLUENT SOCIETY

THE LIBERAL HOUR

ECONOMIC DEVELOPMENT

THE SCOTCH

THE NEW INDUSTRIAL STATE

THE TRIUMPH

INDIAN PAINTING
(WITH MOHINDER SINGH RANDHAWA)

AMBASSADOR'S JOURNAL

ECONOMICS, PEACE AND LAUGHTER

A CHINA PASSAGE

ECONOMICS AND THE PUBLIC PURPOSE

MONEY: WHENCE IT CAME, WHERE IT WENT

THE AGE OF UNCERTAINTY

ALMOST EVERYONE'S GUIDE TO ECONOMICS

THE NATURE OF MASS POVERTY

ANNALS OF AN ABIDING LIBERAL

A LIFE IN OUR TIMES

THE VOICE OF THE POOR

THE ANATOMY OF POWER

A VIEW FROM THE STANDS

ECONOMICS IN PERSPECTIVE:
A CRITICAL HISTORY

CAPITALISM, COMMUNISM AND COEXISTENCE

A TENURED PROFESSOR

THE CULTURE OF CONTENTMENT

A SHORT
HISTORY OF
FINANCIAL
EUPHORIA

John Kenneth
Galbraith

WHITTLE BOOKS
IN ASSOCIATION WITH
VIKING

VIKING
Published by the Penguin Group
Penguin Books USA Inc., 375 Hudson Street, New York, New York 10014,
U.S.A.
Penguin Books Ltd, 27 Wrights Lane, London W8 5TZ, England
Penguin Books Australia Ltd, Ringwood, Victoria, Australia
Penguin Books Canada Ltd, 10 Alcorn Avenue,
Toronto, Ontario, Canada M4V 3B2
Penguin Books (N.Z.) Ltd, 182-190 Wairau Road, Auckland 10, New Zealand

Penguin Books Ltd, Registered Offices: Harmondsworth,
Middlesex, England

Published in 1993 by Viking Penguin,
a division of Penguin Books USA Inc.

1 3 5 7 9 10 8 6 4 2

This book was first published by Whittle Books as part of the Larger Agenda
Series. Reprinted by arrangement with Whittle Communications L.P.

Photographs: Paul M. Warburg, Brown Brothers, page 6; Roger Babson, Culver
Pictures, page 8; railroad construction, courtesy of Union Pacific Museum Collection, page 65; Joseph Schumpeter, the Bettmann Archive, page 67; J. P. Morgan, Culver Pictures, page 68; Charles Ponzi, Brown Brothers, page 73; Florida
land boom, Florida State Archives, page 74; Charles Mitchell, Brown Brothers,
page 76; Irving Fisher, Culver Pictures, page 79; 1929 crash, the Bettmann
Archive, page 82; Bernard Cornfeld, © Michael Crecco/The Picture Group,
page 90; Robert Vesco, AP/Wide World Photos, page 93; 1987 crash,© Susan
Meiselas/Magnum Photos, page 96; Robert Campeau, the Bettmann Archive,
page 103.

Illustrations: Holland tulips, courtesy of W. Graham Arader III, Chicago, page
29; John Law, Culver Pictures, page 35; Robert Harley, Culver Pictures,
page 44; South Sea Company territory map, courtesy of the Newberry Library,
Chicago, page 46; Sir William Phips, Culver Pictures, page 55.

LIBRARY OF CONGRESS CATALOGING-IN-PUBLICATION DATA
Galbraith, John Kenneth
A short history of financial euphoria / John Kenneth Galbraith.
p. cm.
Includes bibliographical references.
ISBN 0-670-85028-4
1. Speculation—Case studies. I. Title
HG4528.G35 1993
332.64'5—dc20
92-50765

Printed in the United States of America
Set in Sabon
Designed by Kathryn Parise

C O N T E N T S

Foreword to the 1993 Edition   vii

1   The Speculative Episode   1

2   The Common Denominators   12

3   The Classic Cases, I: The
Tulipomania; John Law
and the Banque Royale   26

4   The Classic Cases, II:
The Bubble   43

5   The American Tradition   53

6   1929   70

7   October Redux   87

8   Reprise   105

Notes on Sources   111

FOREWORD
TO THE 1993 EDITION

It is now three years since I did the main work on this small book. As I told in the Foreword to the earlier edition, it concerns matters that have interested me for a third of a century and more. I first dealt with them in *The Great Crash, 1929*, published a little after the twenty-fifth anniversary of the 1929 debacle. That book has been continuously available ever since. Whenever it was about to pass out of print, some new speculative episode or disaster would bring it back to public attention. Over a lifetime I have been, in a modest way, a steady beneficiary of the speculative aberration in its association with more than occasional insanity. Only a stalwart character keeps me from welcoming these events as proof of personal prescience and as a source of small financial reward.

In the first Foreword to this volume, I told of my hope that business executives, the inhabitants of the financial world and the citizens of speculative mood, tendency or temptation might be reminded of the way that not only fools but quite a lot of other people are recurrently separated from their money in the moment of speculative euphoria. I am less certain than when I then wrote of the social and personal value of such a warning. Recurrent speculative insanity and the associated financial deprivation and larger devastation are, I am persuaded, inherent in the system. Perhaps it is better that this be recognized and accepted.

In the years since I wrote this short disquisition, the main players in the most recent speculative episode, that of the extravagant eighties, have met their all but inevitable fate, and the larger economic consequences have been made strongly and sadly evident. The list of those who have descended abruptly from the heights is long, and only a few need be mentioned. Mr. Michael Milken, perhaps the most spectacular figure of the last boom and certainly the best paid, is a recent resident in a minimum-security gaol, which, if not wholly uncomfortable, could not have seemed personally rewarding. One supposes that he met each new day without enthusiasm. Mr. Donald Trump is said not to be broke; he was, however, described in recent news accounts as having a negative net worth. These distinctions are no doubt important in the world of finance. The Reichman brothers, with Robert Campeau the Canadian gift to financial excess, are indubitably broke with depressive effect on the banks that were captured by their euphoric mood. Perhaps it is to their credit that, like Donald Trump, they erected monuments that will long commemorate their adventure. In London, tourists going down the Thames to the Tower will extend their journey to encompass the Canary Wharf development, perhaps the most awesome recent example of speculative dementia.

To a marked extent, the speculative orgy of the eighties was in real estate, including that financed through the S & L's by the guaranteeing American taxpayer. Salomon Brothers of Wall Street recently estimated that it will be an average of twelve years before presently empty commercial real estate will be absorbed. Alas for averages. They think it will be an estimated twenty-six years in Boston, forty-six years in New York and fifty-six years down in San Antonio, Texas (the leader, so to speak), in this provision for the future.

However, the effects of the splurge extend far beyond real estate and range from the serious to the sad. New Yorkers can hardly escape a tear when they see the efforts of R. H. Macy, one of their great civic symbols, to stay alive and pay for the goods it sells and the pressing charges of those who supervise it in bankruptcy. The cause of the difficulties of this great institution are not in doubt: it was the heavy load of debt incurred in the effort to obtain and retain control during the years of financial pillage and devastation. Across the country other enterprises were similarly afflicted and are similarly oppressed with the resulting debt. Oppressed with them are the banks that sustained the real estate speculation and provided credit for the mergers and acquisitions, hostile takeovers and leveraged buyouts, and the other exercises in financial devastation.

But there is more. The recession that began in the summer of 1990 and continued so obdurately in face of the weekly predictions of recovery was almost certainly caused and was certainly deepened and prolonged by the speculative collapse. Public confidence was shaken, corporate investment was curtailed, troubled banks were forced to restrict lending, workers were discharged and corporate executives and bureaucrats shed. (One does not fire or sack higher-income personnel; in the interest of greater efficiency, they are only shed.)

The end is not yet. Had there been no speculative excess and collapse with their larger economic effect, the political history of 1992 would have been far different. It was the boom and collapse that ended the political career and presidency of George Bush. Without a recession and with a good or even a moderately performing economy, his reelection would have been certain, a cinch. With Herbert Hoover, Mr. Bush stands as one of two Presidents in this century who were destroyed by Wall Street. In politics, as in other matters, one must beware of one's friends.

Not all, it should be said for Bush, will be bad. John Law, who presided at a magisterial level over the great French boom of the early eighteenth century, went dismally into exile. So did some of those in government office who suffered the South Sea Bubble. By contrast, Mr. Bush, as also Mr. Reagan out in California, will have a wholly civilized retirement. In small ways the history of the great speculative boom and its aftermath does change. Much, much more remains the same.

A
SHORT
HISTORY OF

FINANCIAL
EUPHORIA

C H A P T E R   1

THE SPECULATIVE EPISODE

Anyone taken as an individual is tolerably sensi-
ble and reasonable—as a member of a crowd, he
at once becomes a blockhead.

—FRIEDRICH VON SCHILLER,
AS QUOTED BY BERNARD BARUCH

That the free-enterprise economy is given to recurrent episodes of speculation will be agreed. These—great events and small, involving bank notes, securities, real estate, art, and other assets or objects—are, over the years and centuries, part of history. What have not been sufficiently analyzed are the features common to these episodes, the things that signal their certain return and have thus

the considerable practical value of aiding understanding and prediction. Regulation and
more orthodox economic knowledge are not
what protect the individual and the financial
institution when euphoria returns, leading on
as it does to wonder at the increase in values
and wealth, to the rush to participate that
drives up prices, and to the eventual crash and
its sullen and painful aftermath. There is protection only in a clear perception of the characteristics common to these flights into what
must conservatively be described as mass insanity. Only then is the investor warned and
saved.

There are, however, few matters on which
such a warning is less welcomed. In the short
run, it will be said to be an attack, motivated
by either deficient understanding or uncon-
trolled envy, on the wonderful process of enrichment. More durably, it will be thought to
demonstrate a lack of faith in the inherent
wisdom of the market itself.

The more obvious features of the speculative episode are manifestly clear to anyone
open to understanding. Some artifact or some
development, seemingly new and desirable—
tulips in Holland, gold in Louisiana, real estate in Florida, the superb economic designs

of Ronald Reagan—captures the financial mind or perhaps, more accurately, what so passes. The price of the object of speculation goes up. Securities, land, objets d'art, and other property, when bought today, are worth more tomorrow. This increase and the prospect attract new buyers; the new buyers assure a further increase. Yet more are attracted; yet more buy; the increase continues. The speculation building on itself provides its own momentum.

This process, once it is recognized, is clearly evident, and especially so after the fact. So also, if more subjectively, are the basic attitudes of the participants. These take two forms. There are those who are persuaded that some new price-enhancing circumstance is in control, and they expect the market to stay up and go up, perhaps indefinitely. It is adjusting to a new situation, a new world of greatly, even infinitely increasing returns and resulting values. Then there are those, superficially more astute and generally fewer in number, who perceive or believe themselves to perceive the speculative mood of the moment. They are in to ride the upward wave; their particular genius, they are convinced, will allow them to get out before the speculation runs its course. They will get the maximum reward from the increase as it continues; they will be out before the eventual fall.

For built into this situation is the eventual and inevitable fall. Built in also is the circumstance that it cannot come gently or gradually. When it comes, it bears the grim face of disaster. That is because both of the groups of participants in the speculative situation are programmed for sudden efforts at escape. Something, it matters little what—although it will always be much debated—triggers the ultimate reversal. Those who had been riding the upward wave decide now is the time to get out. Those who thought the increase would be forever find their illusion destroyed abruptly, and they, also, respond to the newly revealed reality by selling or trying to sell. Thus the collapse. And thus the rule, supported by the experience of centuries: the speculative episode always ends not with a whimper but with a bang. There will be occasion to see the operation of this rule frequently repeated.

So much, as I've said, is clear. Less understood is the mass psychology of the speculative mood. When it is fully comprehended, it allows those so favored to save themselves from disaster. Given the pressure of this crowd psychology, however, the saved will be the exception to a very broad and binding rule. They will be required to resist two compelling forces: one, the powerful personal interest that develops in the euphoric belief, and the other, the pressure of public and seemingly superior financial opinion that is brought to bear on behalf of such belief. Both stand as proof of Schiller's dictum that the crowd converts the individual from reasonably good sense to the stupidity against which, as he also said, "the very Gods Themselves contend in vain."

Although only a few observers have noted the vested interest in error that accompanies speculative euphoria, it is, nonetheless, an extremely plausible phenomenon. Those involved with the speculation are experiencing an increase in wealth—getting rich or being further enriched. No one wishes to believe that this is fortuitous or undeserved; all wish to think that it is the result of their own superior insight or intuition. The very increase in values thus captures the thoughts and minds of those being rewarded. Speculation buys up, in a very practical way, the intelligence of those involved.

This is particularly true of the first group

noted above—those who are convinced that values are going up permanently and indefinitely. But the errors of vanity of those who think they will beat the speculative game are also thus reinforced. As long as they are in, they have a strong pecuniary commitment to belief in the unique personal intelligence that tells them there will be yet more. In the last century, one of the most astute observers of the euphoric episodes common to those years was Walter Bagehot, financial writer and early editor of *The Economist.* To him we are indebted for the observation that "all people are most credulous when they are most happy."

Fellow bankers and the investment houses in 1929 assailed Paul M. Warburg, a banker and founder of the Federal Reserve System, for his warnings of a crash.

Strongly reinforcing the vested interest in euphoria is the condemnation that the reputable public and financial opinion directs at those who express doubt or dissent. It is said that they are unable, because of defective imagination or other mental inadequacy, to grasp the new and rewarding circumstances that sustain and secure the increase in values. Or their motivation is deeply suspect. In the winter of 1929, Paul M. Warburg, the most respected banker of his time and one of the founding parents of the Federal Reserve System, spoke critically of the then-current orgy of "unrestrained speculation" and said that if it continued, there would ultimately be a disastrous collapse, and the country would face a serious depression. The reaction to his statement was bitter, even vicious. He was held to be obsolete in his views; he was "sandbagging American prosperity"; quite possibly, he was himself short in the market. There was more than a shadow of anti-Semitism in this response.

Later, in September of that year, Roger Babson, a considerable figure of the time who was diversely interested in statistics, market forecasting, economics, theology, and the law of gravity, specifically foresaw a crash and said, "it may be terrific." There would be a 60- to 80-point drop in the Dow, and, in consequence, "factories will shut down...men will be thrown out of work...the vicious circle will get in full swing and the result will be a serious business depression."

Babson's forecast caused a sharp break in the market, and the reaction to it was even more furious than that to Warburg's. *Barron's*

Economist Roger Babson's forecast of the crash of 1929 brought him grave rebuke from the great financial houses of the time.

said he should not be taken seriously by anyone acquainted with the "notorious inaccuracy" of his past statements. The great New York Stock Exchange house of Hornblower and Weeks told its customers, in a remarkably resonant sentence, that "we would not be stampeded into selling stocks because of a gratuitous forecast of a bad break in the market by a well-known statistician." Even Professor Irving Fisher of Yale University, a pioneer in the construction of index numbers, and otherwise the most innovative economist of his day, spoke out sharply against Babson. It was a lesson to all to keep quiet and give tacit support to those indulging their euphoric vision.

Without, I hope, risking too grave a charge of self-gratification, I might here cite personal experience. In the late winter of 1955, J. William Fulbright, then the chairman of the Senate Banking and Currency Committee, called hearings to consider a modest speculative buildup in the securities market. Along with Bernard Baruch, the current head of the New York Stock Exchange, and other authorities real or alleged, I was invited to testify. I refrained from predicting a crash, contented myself with reminding the committee at some length as to what had happened a quarter of a century earlier, and urged a substantial protective increase in margin requirements—down payments on the purchases of stocks. While I was testifying, the market took a considerable tumble.

The reaction in the next days was severe. The postman each morning staggered in with a load of letters condemning my comments, the most extreme threatening what the CIA was later to call executive action, the mildest saying that prayers were being offered for my richly deserved demise. A few days later I broke my leg in a skiing accident, and newsmen, seeing me in a cast, reported the fact. Letters now came in from speculators saying their prayers had been answered. In a small way I had done something for religion. I posted the most compelling of the communications in a seminar room at Harvard as an instruction to the young. Presently the market recovered, and my mail returned to normal.

On a more immediately relevant occasion, in the autumn of 1986, my attention became focused on the speculative buildup then tak-

ing place in the stock market, the casino manifestations in program and index trading, and
the related enthusiasms emanating from corporate raiding, leveraged buyouts, and the
mergers-and-acquisitions mania. *The New
York Times* asked me to write an article on
the subject; I more than willingly complied.

Sadly, when my treatise was completed, it
was thought by the *Times* editors to be too
alarming. I had made clear that the markets
were in one of their classically euphoric moods
and said that a crash was inevitable, while
thoughtfully avoiding any prediction as to
precisely when. In early 1987, the *Atlantic*
published with pleasure what the *Times* had
declined. (The *Times* later relented and
arranged with the *Atlantic* editors for publica-
tion of an interview that covered much of the
same ground.) However, until the crash of
October 19 of that year, the response to the
piece was both sparse and unfavorable.
"Galbraith doesn't like to see people making
money" was one of the more corroding obser-
vations. After October 19, however, almost
everyone I met told me that he had read and
admired the article; on the day of the crash itself, some 40 journalists and television com-
mentators from Tokyo, across the United

States, and on to Paris and Milan called me for comment. Clearly, given the nature of the euphoric mood and the vested interest therein, the critic must wait until after the crash for any approval, not to say applause.

To summarize: The euphoric episode is protected and sustained by the will of those who are involved, in order to justify the circumstances that are making them rich. And it is equally protected by the will to ignore, exorcise, or condemn those who express doubts.

Before going on to look at the great speculations of the past, I would like further to identify the forces that initiate, sustain, and otherwise characterize the speculative episode and which, when they recur, always evoke surprise, wonder, and enthusiasm anew. All this we will then see in nearly invariant form occurring again and again in the history I here record.

CHAPTER 2

THE COMMON
DENOMINATORS

In the chapters that follow, I review the great
speculative episodes of the past—of the last
three centuries. As already observed, common
features recur. This is of no slight practical
importance; recognizing them, the sensible
person or institution is or should be warned.
And perhaps some will be. But as the previous
chapter indicates, the chances are not great,
for built into the speculative episode is the euphoria, the mass escape from reality, that excludes any serious contemplation of the true
nature of what is taking place.

Contributing to and supporting this euphoria are two further factors little noted in our

time or in past times. The first is the extreme brevity of the financial memory. In consequence, financial disaster is quickly forgotten. In further consequence, when the same or closely similar circumstances occur again, sometimes in only a few years, they are hailed by a new, often youthful, and always supremely self-confident generation as a brilliantly innovative discovery in the financial and larger economic world. There can be few fields of human endeavor in which history counts for so little as in the world of finance. Past experience, to the extent that it is part of memory at all, is dismissed as the primitive refuge of those who do not have the insight to appreciate the incredible wonders of the present.

The second factor contributing to speculative euphoria and programmed collapse is the specious association of money and intelligence. Mention of this is not a formula for eliciting reputable applause, but, alas, it must be accepted, for acceptance is also highly useful, a major protection against personal or institutional disaster.

The basic situation is wonderfully clear. In all free-enterprise (once called capitalist) attitudes there is a strong tendency to believe that the more money, either as income or assets, of which an individual is possessed or with which he is associated, the deeper and more compelling his economic and social perception, the more astute and penetrating his mental processes. Money is the measure of capitalist achievement. The more money, the greater the achievement and the intelligence that supports it.

Further, in a world where for many the acquisition of money is difficult and the resulting sums palpably insufficient, the possession of it in large amount seems a miracle. Accordingly, possession must be associated with some special genius. This view is then reinforced by the air of self-confidence and self-approval that is commonly assumed by the affluent. On no matter is the mental inferiority of the ordinary layman so rudely and abruptly stated: "I'm afraid that you simply don't understand financial matters." In fact, such reverence for the possession of money again indicates the shortness of memory, the ignorance of history, and the consequent capacity for self- and popular delusion just mentioned. Having money may mean, as often in the past and frequently in the present, that the person is foolishly indifferent to legal constraints and may, in modern times, be a potential resident of a minimum-security prison. Or the money may have been inherited, and, notoriously, mental acuity does not pass in reliable fashion from parent to offspring. On all these matters, a more careful examination of the presumed financial genius, a sternly detailed interrogation to test his or her intelligence, would frequently and perhaps normally produce a different conclusion. Unfortunately the subject is rarely available for such scrutiny; that, too, wealth or seeming financial competence often excludes.

Finally and more specifically, we compulsively associate unusual intelligence with the leadership of the great financial institutions— the large banking, investment-banking, insurance, and brokerage houses. The larger the capital assets and income flow controlled, the deeper the presumed financial, economic, and social perception.

In practice, the individual or individuals at the top of these institutions are often there because, as happens regularly in great organizations, theirs was mentally the most predictable and, in consequence, bureaucratically the least inimical of the contending talent. He, she, or they are then endowed with the authority that encourages acquiescence from their subordinates and applause from their acolytes and that excludes adverse opinion or criticism. They are thus admirably protected in what may be a serious commitment to error.

Another factor is at work here. Those with money to lend are, by long force of habit, tradition, and more especially the needs and desires of borrowers, accorded a special measure of deference in daily routine. This is readily transmuted by the recipient into an assurance of personal mental superiority. Treated that way, I must be wise. In consequence, self-scrutiny—the greatest support to minimal good sense—is at risk.

This is no exercise in idle theory. In the 1970s, it was the greatest of the New York banks and bankers that, praising their own success in recycling Arab oil revenues, made those durably unfortunate loans to Latin America and to Africa and Poland. It was intellectually questionable men in intimate and protected association with large assets who fed money through the ridiculous Penn Square Bank in Oklahoma City to the outstretched hands in the neighboring oil patch. And in

Dallas and Houston to the manifold disasters

of the great Texas oil and real estate speculations. And who, across the country in the 1980s, initiated and exploited the terrible savings and loan debacle.

In the chapters that follow, we will see, and repeatedly, how the investing public is fascinated and captured by the great financial mind. That fascination derives, in turn, from the scale of the financial operations and the feeling that, with so much money involved, the mental resources behind them cannot be less.

Only after the speculative collapse does the truth emerge. What was thought to be unusual acuity turns out to be only a fortuitous and unfortunate association with the assets. Over the long years of history, the result for those who have been thus misjudged (including, invariably, by themselves) has been opprobrium followed by personal disgrace or a retreat into the deeper folds of obscurity. Or it has been exile, suicide, or, in modern times, at least moderately uncomfortable confinement. The rule will often be here reiterated: *financial genius is before the fall.*

I turn now to specific features of the speculative episode.

■

Uniformly in all such events there is the thought that there is something new in the world. It can, as we shall see, be one of the many things. In the 17th century it was the arrival of the tulips in Western Europe, as the next chapter will tell. Later it was the seeming wonders of the joint-stock company, now called the corporation. More recently, in the United States, prior to the great crash of 1987 (often referred to more benignly as a melt-down), it was the accommodation of the markets to the confident, free-enterprise vision of Ronald Reagan with the companion release of the economy from the heavy hand of government and the associated taxes, antitrust enforcement, and regulation. Contributing was the rediscovery, as reliably before, of leverage, in this case the miracle of high-risk or junk bonds supporting the initiatives of the new generation of corporate raiders and leveraged-buyout specialists.

In all speculative episodes there is always an element of pride in discovering what is seemingly new and greatly rewarding in the way of financial instrument or investment opportunity. The individual or institution that does so is thought to be wonderfully ahead of the mob. This insight is then confirmed as others rush to exploit their own, only slightly later vision. This perception of something new and exceptional rewards the ego of the participant, as it is expected also to reward his or her pocketbook. And for a while it does.

As to new financial instruments, however, experience establishes a firm rule, and on few economic matters is understanding more important and frequently, indeed, more slight. The rule is that financial operations do not lend themselves to innovation. What is recurrently so described and celebrated is, without exception, a small variation on an established design, one that owes its distinctive character to the aforementioned brevity of the financial memory. The world of finance hails the invention of the wheel over and over again, often in a slightly more unstable version. All financial innovation involves, in one form or another, the creation of debt secured in greater or lesser adequacy by real assets. This was true in one of the earliest seeming marvels: when banks discovered that they could print bank notes and issue them to borrowers in a volume in excess of the hard-money deposits in the banks' strong rooms.

The depositors could be counted upon, it was believed or hoped, not to come all at once for their money. There was no seeming limit to the debt that could thus be leveraged on a given volume of hard cash. A wonderful thing. The limit became apparent, however, when some alarming news, perhaps of the extent of the leverage itself, caused too many of the original depositors to want their money at the same time. All subsequent financial innovation has involved similar debt creation leveraged against more limited assets with only modifications in the earlier design. All crises have involved debt that, in one fashion or another, has become dangerously out of scale in relation to the underlying means of payment.

More often, even a semblance of innovation is absent. In the 1920s, as we shall see, great holding companies were created. The owners, that is to say the stockholders, issued bonds and preferred stock in order to buy other stocks. As the latter appreciated in value—for a while—all the increase accrued to the owners. This was proclaimed one of the financial miracles of that age. It was, in fact, leverage in, at most, a slightly different guise.

In the 1980s, in what came to be called the mergers-and-acquisitions mania, corporate raiders and their investment-banking acolytes issued bonds in great volume against the credit of the companies being taken over. Or the managements thus threatened similarly issued bonds to buy and retire the stock of their own companies and so retain control. It was, once again, a time of presumed innovation and adventure. In reality, this was again only the reappearance of leverage; not even the terminology was new.

The bonds so issued, it might be added, carried high interest rates that were meant to compensate for the risk incurred. For a time, this too was considered a major new discovery despite the rather adverse appellation accorded these financial instruments, namely junk bonds. Michael Milken of the investment house of Drexel Burnham Lambert, sponsor beyond equal of junk-bond issues, was hailed as an innovator in the field of finance. His income of $550 million in 1987 was thought appropriate compensation for so inventive a figure, one of Edisonian stature. Mr. Milken's competence and superior diligence as a salesman, sometimes called promoter, is not in doubt, but the discovery that high-risk bonds leveraged on limited assets should have a higher interest rate hardly stands on a par as an invention with the electric light. Again the wheel, here in an especially fragile version.

The final and common feature of the speculative episode—in stock markets, real estate, art, or junk bonds—is what happens after the inevitable crash. This, invariably, will be a time of anger and recrimination and also of profoundly unsubtle introspection. The anger will fix upon the individuals who were previously most admired for their financial imagination and acuity. Some of them, having been persuaded of their own exemption from confining orthodoxy, will, as noted, have gone beyond the law, and their fall and, occasionally, their incarceration will now be viewed with righteous satisfaction.

There will also be scrutiny of the previously much-praised financial instruments and practices—paper money; implausible securities issues; insider trading; market rigging; more recently, program and index trading— that have facilitated and financed the speculation. There will be talk of regulation and reform. What will not be discussed is the speculation itself or the aberrant optimism that lay behind it. Nothing is more remarkable than this: in the aftermath of speculation, the reality will be all but ignored.

There are two reasons for this. In the first place, many people and institutions have been involved, and whereas it is acceptable to attribute error, gullibility, and excess to a single individual or even to a particular corporation, it is not deemed fitting to attribute them to a whole community, and certainly not to the whole financial community. Widespread naiveté, even stupidity, is manifest; mention of this, however, runs drastically counter to the earlier-noted presumption that intelligence is intimately associated with money. The financial community must be assumed to be intellectually above such extravagance of error.

The second reason that the speculative mood and mania are exempted from blame is theological. In accepted free-enterprise attitudes and doctrine, the market is a neutral and accurate reflection of external influences; it is not supposed to be subject to an inherent and internal dynamic of error. This is the classical faith. So there is a need to find some cause for the crash, however farfetched, that is external to the market itself. Or some abuse of the market that has inhibited its normal performance.

Again, this is no matter of idle theory; there are very practical consequences, and these, as we shall see, are especially evident and important in our own time. That the months and years before the 1987 stock-market crash were characterized by intense speculation no one would seriously deny. But in the aftermath of that crash, little or no importance was attributed to this speculation. Instead, the deficit in the federal budget became the decisive factor. The escape from reality continued with studies by the New York Stock Exchange, the Securities and Exchange Commission, and a special presidential commission, all of which passed over or minimized the speculation as a conditioning cause. Markets in our culture are a totem; to them can be ascribed no inherent aberrant tendency or fault.

There is ample reason to be interested in the history of speculative excess and its effects for its own sake. One relishes, especially if from afar, the drama of mass insanity. There is a rewarding sense of personal foresight in knowing of the invariable end of each episode. But there is also a high practical utility in observing how reliably the common features just cited recur. Seeing the earlier of the symptoms reemerge, as they will, there is a chance—a slim chance, to be sure, given the sweeping power of financial euphoria—that otherwise vulnerable individuals will be warned. To this end, I now turn to the great speculative episodes of the past and their common features.

CHAPTER 3

THE CLASSIC CASES, I: THE TULIPOMANIA; JOHN LAW AND THE BANQUE ROYALE

Speculators may do no harm as bubbles on a steady stream of enterprise. But the position is serious when enterprise becomes the bubble on a whirlpool of speculation.

—JOHN MAYNARD KEYNES,
*The General Theory of
Employment Interest and Money*

That there were speculative episodes going back to the days of the Florentines and the Venetians none can doubt. Fernand Braudel, the French economic historian and ultimate authority on these matters, has noted that there were active securities markets in Genoa, Florence, and Venice as early as the 14th century, and long before then there was active trading in coinage and commodities, with, almost certainly, purchase and sale based not on present but on imagined prospective value.

The first modern stock market—modern especially as to the volume of transactions—appeared, however, in Amsterdam at the beginning of the 17th century. And it was in the stable, wide-horizoned land of the Dutch, with its stable and somber people, that there came in the 1630s the first of the great speculative explosions known to history. It remains to this day one of the most remarkable. It was not, however, in stock-market offerings or in real estate or, as one might have expected, in the superb Dutch paintings; the speculation was in tulip bulbs, and it has come down over the last 350 years with a name of its own—the Tulipomania.

The tulip—*Tulipa* of the lily family Liliaceae, of which there are around 160 species—grows wild in the eastern Mediterranean countries and on east from there. The bulbs first came to Western Europe in the 16th century; a cargo of them that arrived in

Antwerp from Constantinople in 1562 is thought to have been especially important in spreading knowledge and appreciation of the flower. This appreciation became, in time, very great; enormous prestige was soon attached to the possession and cultivation of the plant.

Speculation, it has been noted, comes when popular imagination settles on something seemingly new in the field of commerce or finance. The tulip, beautiful and varied in its colors, was one of the first things so to serve. To this day it remains one of the more unusual of such instruments. Nothing more improbable ever contributed so wonderfully to the mass delusion here examined.

Attention came to be concentrated on the possession and display of the more esoteric of the blooms. And appreciation of the more exceptional of the flowers rapidly gave way to a yet deeper appreciation of the increase in the price that their beauty and rarity were commanding. For this the bulbs were now bought, and by the mid-1630s the increase seemed to be without limit.

The rush to invest engulfed the whole of Holland. No person of minimal sensitivity of mind felt that he could be left behind. Prices

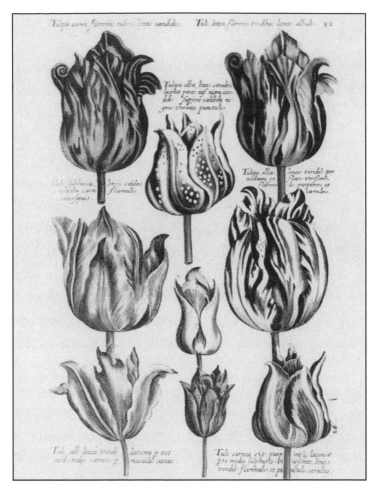

When Johann Theodore de Bry created this copper-plate engraving in 1611 for a botanical book on new flowers called *Florilegium Novum,* he would have had little inkling that some of the bulbs would be worth $25,000 to $50,000 a mere 20 years later.

were extravagant; by 1636, a bulb of no previously apparent worth might be exchanged for "a new carriage, two grey horses and a complete harness."

The speculation became more and more intense. A bulb might now change hands several times at steadily increasing and wonderfully rewarding prices while still unseen in the ground. And there were also some terrible accidents. Charles Mackay, in *Extraordinary Popular Delusions and the Madness of Crowds,* his classic book on speculation (and other departures from reason), tells gleefully a story first told in Blainville's *Travels,* that of a young sailor who, for bringing word of a shipment of goods from the Levant, was rewarded by a merchant with a fine red herring for his breakfast. Presently the merchant, who was much involved in the tulip speculation, found missing a bulb of a *Semper Augustus* worth some 3,000 florins, an unimaginable $25,000 to $50,000 today. When he sought out the sailor to question him, the latter was discovered contentedly finishing the onion, as he had supposed it to be, along with the fish.

In an especially memorable passage, Mackay tells of the mood of the country as the speculation continued:

The demand for tulips of a rare species increased so much in the year 1636, that regular marts for their sale were established on the Stock Exchange of Amsterdam, in Rotterdam, Harlaem, Leyden, Alkmar, Hoorn, and other towns.... At first, as in all these gambling mania, confidence was at its height, and every body gained. The tulip-jobbers speculated in the rise and fall of the tulip stocks, and made large profits by buying when prices fell, and selling out when they rose. Many individuals grew suddenly rich. A golden bait hung temptingly out before the people, and one after the other, they rushed to the tulip-marts, like flies around a honey-pot. Every one imagined that the passion for tulips would last for ever, and that the wealthy from every part of the world would send to Holland, and pay whatever prices were asked for them. The riches of Europe would be concentrated on the shores of the Zuyder Zee, and poverty banished from the favored clime of Holland. Nobles, citizens, farmers, mechanics, seamen, footmen, maid-servants, even chimney-sweeps and old clotheswomen, dabbled in tulips. People of all grades converted their property into cash, and invested it in flowers. Houses and lands were offered for sale at ruinously low prices, or assigned in payment of bargains made at the tulip-mart. Foreigners became smitten with the same frenzy, and money poured into Holland from all directions. The prices of the necessaries of life rose again by degrees: houses and lands, horses and carriages, and luxuries of every sort, rose in value with them, and for some months Holland seemed the very antechamber of Plutus. The operations of the trade became so extensive and so intricate, that it was found necessary to draw up a code of laws for the guidance of the dealers.... In the smaller towns, where there was no exchange, the principal tavern was usually selected as the "show-place," where high and low traded in tulips and confirmed their bargains over sumptuous entertainments. These dinners were sometimes attended by two or three hundred persons, and large vases of tulips, in full bloom, were placed at regular intervals upon the tables and sideboards for their gratification during the repast.

It was wonderful; never in their history had the Dutch seemed so favored. In keeping with the immutable rules governing such episodes, each upsurge in prices persuaded more speculators to participate. This justified the hopes of those already participating, paving the way for yet further action and increase, and so assuring yet more and ever-continued enrichment. Money was borrowed for purchase; the small bulbs leveraged large loans.

In 1637 came the end. Again the controlling rules were in command. The wise and the nervous began to detach, no one knows for what reason; others saw them go; the rush to sell became a panic; the prices dropped as if over a precipice. Those who had purchased, many by pledging property for credit—here the leverage—were suddenly bereft or bankrupt. "Substantial merchants were reduced almost to beggary, and many a representative of a noble line saw the fortunes of his house ruined beyond redemption," according to Mackay.

In the aftermath, the bitterness, recrimination, and search for scapegoats—all normal— were extreme, as was the avoidance of mention of the mass mania that was the true cause. Those who had contracted to buy at the enormously inflated prices defaulted en masse. Angry sellers sought enforcement of their contracts of sale; the courts, identifying it as a gambling operation, were unhelpful. Not less than with the failing banks and savings and loan associations in recent times, the state then emerged as the recourse of last resort. Alas, the only remedy would have been to restore the price of the bulbs to the pre-crash level, but this was manifestly impractical, and so the so recently rich were left with their loss.

Nor were they alone in misfortune. The collapse of the tulip prices and the resulting impoverishment had a chilling effect on Dutch economic life in the years that followed—there ensued, in modern terminology, an appreciable depression. There was one mitigating result: the cultivation of the tulip continued in Holland, and wide markets eventually developed for flowers and bulbs. Anyone who has seen the tulip fields of this calm and pleasant land in the spring retains forever a feeling that the Tulipomania did foretell nature's true grace.

Missing from the history of the Tulipomania and the predictable circumstances associated with it, as with all great speculations, are the names of the major players. We are more fortunate in the next of the classic episodes; it is dominated by one of the central figures in all financial history, that of the Scotsman John Law.

But even in the case of Law, a word of caution is in order. I have sufficiently urged that all suggestions as to financial innovation be regarded with extreme skepticism. Such seeming innovation is merely some variant on an old design, new only in the brief and defective memory of the financial world. No one over the

John Law's scheme to pay off France's debts by selling shares in the nonexistent gold riches of Louisiana ended in ruin.

centuries has been more celebrated than John Law; the *Encyclopaedia Britannica* declares him to have been both an honest man and a financial genius. In his case too, however, let there be doubts.

Law was born in 1671 into the world of finance. His father, an Edinburgh goldsmith, was, in the manner of men in that trade, actively engaged in holding and lending money. The younger Law moved at an early age to London, where, along with enjoying a markedly sybaritic existence, he seems to have given some attention to matters of banking and finance. However, this education was drastically interrupted in 1694, when, on a field adjacent to central London in what is now Bloomsbury, he was unduly successful in a duel. For bringing his opponent down with a sword "to his belly," he was arrested and clapped into jail on a murder charge. After lengthy proceedings, the matter was resolved by his escape from prison, it is thought with some official connivance. He made his way to the Continent, where for the next several years he evidently made his living as a highly resourceful gambler. His winnings, it is said, were the result of his having worked out the odds in a contemporary version of craps— something that would now have him barred from the tables.

In the Netherlands he also observed the operations of the great and successful Bank of Amsterdam and gave thought to banking and to the idea of a land bank that would take over landed property and issue notes secured by the real estate as loans. Just how the land would be redeemed by noteholders was uncertain. The idea was, however, important for his future career in Paris. There he arrived in 1716 after a brief return to Scotland, where he sought to promote his schemes, only to have them rather decisively and, none can doubt, very wisely rejected.

Paris was more amenable or, more precisely, more unfortunate. It was a propitious moment; Louis XIV had died the year before, leaving two legacies that would prove to be important for Law. One was the Regent for the young Louis XV: Philippe II, Duc d'Orléans, was a man who combined a negligible intellect with deeply committed self-indulgence. The other was a bankrupt treasury and numerous debts deriving from the Sun King's persistent wars and civil extravagance and the extensive corruption among the tax farmers assigned to the raising of the revenues. To both of these opportunities Law addressed himself.

On May 2, 1716, he was accorded the right to establish a bank, which eventually became the Banque Royale, with a capital of six million livres. Included was authorization to issue notes, which were then used by the bank to pay current government expenses and to take over past government debts. The notes, in principle exchangeable into hard coin if one wished, were well received. Some being well received, more were issued.

What was needed, obviously, was a source of earnings in hard cash that would bring in revenues to support the note issue. This was provided in theory by the organization of the Mississippi Company (the Compagnie d'Occident)—later, with larger trading privileges, the Company of the Indies—to pursue the gold deposits that were presumed to exist in the great North American territory of Louisiana. There was no evidence of the gold, but this, as ever in such episodes, was no time for doubters or doubting. Shares of the company were offered to the public, and the response was sensational. The old bourse in the Rue Quincampoix was the scene of the most intense, even riotous, operations in all the history of financial greed. Eventually selling and trading were moved to the more spacious Place Vendôme and on to the neighborhood of the Hôtel de Soissons. So determined were some women purchasers that, in an interesting modern touch, they offered themselves for the right to buy shares. In the 1980s, in a slight variation, some vulnerable clients of Michael Milken and Drexel Burnham Lambert who attended the annual Predators' Balls, as they were denoted, at the Beverly Hills Hotel were said to have had the attention of appropriately ascetic prostitutes. This was meant to encourage them in the purchase

of junk bonds, many of which were comparable in prospect to the shares in the Compagnie d'Occident.

The proceeds of the sale of the stock in the Mississippi Company went not to search for the as yet undiscovered gold, but to the government for its debts. The notes that went out to pay the debt came back to buy more stock. More stock was then issued to satisfy more of the intense demand, the latter having the effect of lifting both the old and the new issues to ever more extravagant heights. All the notes in this highly literal circulation were, it was presumed, backed by coin in the Banque Royale, but the amount of the coin that so sustained the notes was soon minuscule in relation to the volume of paper. Here was leverage in a particularly wondrous form.

In 1720, the end came. The leverage went sharply into reverse, as was to be the experience in a hundred such occurrences, great and small, in the next 250 years. The precipitating factor, it is said, was the decision of the Prince de Conti, annoyed by his inability to buy stock, to send his notes to the Banque Royale to be turned in for gold. According to highly improbable legend, three wagons carried the metal back to him, but the Regent then intervened at Law's request and ordered the Prince to return it all. Meanwhile others were seized by the thought that gold might be better than notes. To restore confidence and assure noteholders and investors that a goodly supply of the metal would be forthcoming, a battalion of Paris mendicants was recruited, and the members were equipped with shovels and marched through the streets of Paris as though on the way to mine the metal in Louisiana. It was thought somewhat distressing when, in the next weeks, many of them were seen back at their old haunts. Whatever the facts, there was a run on the bank—people seeking to convert their notes not into the stock of the Mississippi Company but into gold. On one July day in 1720, 15 people lost their lives in the crush in front of the Banque Royale. The notes were declared no longer convertible. Values, and not just those of the Mississippi stock, collapsed. Citizens who a week before had been millionaires—an indispensable term that was given to us by these years—were now impoverished.

Next came the predictable anger, the search for the individual or institution to be blamed. The search did not have far to go. In the preceding months a grateful sovereign had raised the foreigner, gambler, and escaped murderer

John Law to the highest public post in the kingdom, where, in fact, he instituted some useful economic and tax reforms: idle lands of the clergy were given to the peasants, local tolls were abolished, and tariffs reduced. He had also become Comptroller General of France and had been made the Duc d'Arkansas, a title one wishes might have survived. Now John Law became the object of the most venomous condemnation. Protected by the Regent, he got out of France and spent four years in England, where he was granted amnesty on the murder charge against him. He then went on to Venice, where for the time that remained to him, according to the Duc de Saint-Simon, he "lived, in decent poverty, a quiet and virtuous life, died there in the Catholic faith, piously receiving the Sacraments of the Church."

It is possible to see here again the constants in these matters. Associated with the wealth of the Banque Royale, Law was a genius— intelligence, as ever, derived from association with money. When the wealth dissolved and disappeared, he was a fugitive mercilessly reviled. That Law had a captivating self-assurance seems certain, and this served him well with the Regent and the Parisian public. That what he did, however, was either highly original or minimally sensible is gravely in doubt. Men of genius do not destroy themselves along with so many others and invite such a dismal end.

In the aftermath, as in Holland after the tulips, the French economy was depressed, and economic and financial life was generally disordered—in the slightly exaggerated words of Saint-Simon, with "a tiny minority enriched by the total ruin of all the rest of the people." But, as in Holland and as with superb consistency throughout this history, blame did not fall on the speculation and its gulled participants. It was, as already indicated, John Law who was deemed responsible, as was his Banque Royale, and for a century in France banks would be regarded with suspicion. Those who had lost their minds as well as their money and made the speculation spared themselves all censure.

CHAPTER 4

THE CLASSIC
CASES, II: THE BUBBLE

As the great speculation was coming to its un-
predicted but wholly predictable climax in
Paris in 1720, so was another, this one in
London. Insanity born of optimism and self-
serving illusion was the tale of two cities. As
might be expected, both the British players
and the event itself lacked the French style. It
was, by comparison, a rather ordinary, if exceptionally intense, boom and collapse in securities prices augmented by a comprehensive
exercise in official bribery, corruption, and
chicane.

The discovery that justified the boom, or,
as always and more precisely, the rediscovery,

Robert Harley, Earl of Oxford, helped to found the ill-fated South Sea Company.

was of the joint-stock company. Such companies went back a hundred years and more in England; suddenly, nonetheless, they now emerged as the new wonder of finance and the whole economic world.

In the early years of the 18th century, there had been some notably imaginative stock promotions or proposals—a company to build and market a typewriter, an enterprise considerably ahead of its time; a project for a subtle machine gun that could fire both round and square bullets, depending on whether the enemy was a Christian or a Turk; a project for a mechanical piano. "I can measure the motions of bodies," Sir Isaac Newton once observed, "but I cannot measure human folly." Nor could he do so as regards his own. He was to lose £20,000, now a million dollars and much more, in the speculative orgy that was to come.

The South Sea Company was born in 1711 at the instigation or, perhaps more precisely, as the inspiration of Robert Harley, Earl of Oxford, who was joined in the early years of the enterprise by one John Blunt, a scrivener by profession accomplished in the copying of legal documents and not less in learning of their contents.

Its origins closely resembled those of the Banque Royale and the Mississippi Company; it similarly provided a seeming and undeniably welcome solution to the problem of floating and pressing government debt that, as in France, had been incurred in previous years in the War of the Spanish Succession. In return for its charter, the South Sea Company took over and consolidated this diverse government debt. It was paid interest by the government at the rate of 6 percent and in return received the right to issue stock and to have "the sole trade and traffick, from 1 August 1711, into unto and from the Kingdoms, Lands etc. of America, on the east side from the river Aranoca, to the southernmost part of the Terra del Fuego...." Added was all trade on the western side of the Americas and "into unto and from all countries in the same limits, reputed to belong to the Crown of Spain, or which shall hereafter be discovered."

This map by cartographer Herman Moll was commissioned by the South Sea Company. The entire region displayed, with the exception of Brazil, was claimed as the company's trading territory. Disregarded was the fact that Spain claimed the same territory.

Thoughtfully overlooked was the fact that Spain claimed a monopoly over all truck and trade with this great region, although there was some distant hope that treaty negotiations then under way would accord Britain access to the fabled metallic wealth of Mexico, Peru, and the rest. There would be opportunities in the slave trade; for this, the British operators thought themselves to have a special aptitude.

In the end, a small—very small—window of opportunity did open. Spain briefly allowed the company exactly one voyage a year, subject to a share in its profits. Hope for something better was then partly sustained by the thought that sovereignty over Gibraltar might be traded for greater access to the Americas. The question of that sovereignty was, unfortunately, to remain in contention between Britain and Spain for another two and a half centuries and more.

It would be hard, in fact, to imagine a commercial project that was more questionable. But here, as in Paris, it was not a time for questions. Further issues of stock in return for further assumptions of the public debt were authorized and offered to the public, and, early in 1720, the whole public debt was assumed. Such were the presumed advantages of the enterprise. The legislation was facilitated by the endowment of gifts of the South Sea stock to key ministers of the government, and also by the happy circumstance that several directors of the enterprise sat in Parliament, with an excellent chance, in consequence, to make known therein the great prospects awaiting the company. The latter's directors were also generous in awarding stock to themselves.

In 1720, the British public, or rather that part susceptible to the thought of financial enrichment, responded powerfully to the seeming opportunity presented by the South Seas and yet more to the upward thrust of the stock and the desire to have a part in the gains. The war had enriched a small but significant sector of the British population. The landed and aristocratic classes, though contemptuous of those "in trade" or otherwise concerned with money-making, were also able to surmount their pride and come aboard—money often has that effect. The scenes in the Rue Quincampoix were now repeated in the streets and alleys of the City; the stock of the company, which had been at around £128 in January 1720, went to £330 in March, £550 in May, £890 in June, and to around £1,000 later in the summer. Not before in the kingdom, and perhaps not even in

Paris or Holland, had so many so suddenly become so rich. As ever, the sight of some becoming so effortlessly affluent brought the rush to participate that further powered the upward thrust.

Nor was the South Sea Company the only opportunity. Its success spawned at least a hundred imitators and hitchhikers, all hoping to take part in the boom. These included companies to develop perpetual motion (also ahead of its time), to insure horses, to improve the art of making soap, to trade in hair, to repair and rebuild parsonage and vicarage houses, to transmute quicksilver into malleable fine metal, and to erect houses or hospitals for taking in and maintaining illegitimate children, as well as the immortal enterprise "for carrying on an undertaking of great advantage, but nobody to know what it is." In July of 1720, the government finally called a halt; legislation—the Bubble Act—was passed prohibiting these other promotions, less, it has always been thought, to protect the foolish and the innocent than to secure the speculative monopoly of the South Sea Company itself.

However, by this time the end of that company was in sight. The stock went into a tailspin, partly, without doubt, the result of inspired profit-taking by those inside and at the top. By September it was down to £175, by December to £124. Heroic efforts, rhetorical and otherwise, were made to sustain and revive confidence, including an appeal for help to the newly formed Bank of England. Eventually, with some support from the government, shares leveled off at around £140, approximately one-seventh of their peak value. As before and later, once the crash comes, it overrides all efforts to reverse the disaster.

There soon followed the search for scapegoats; it was fierce, even brutal. Blunt, by now Sir John Blunt, narrowly escaped death when an assailant, presumably a victim, sought to shoot him down in a London street. He later saved himself by turning in to the government his fellow conspirators in high places—a common modern design. Individuals associated with the company were expelled from Parliament, and directors and other officials (including Blunt) had their money and estates confiscated to provide some compensation to the losers. Robert Knight, the company's treasurer, departed suddenly for the Continent, was pursued and imprisoned and his extradition sought. He managed to escape and lived in exile for the next 21 years. James Craggs, an influential elder statesman of the affair, committed suicide. Others went to jail. As in the aftermath of the tulips and of John Law, the economic life of the City of London and that of the country as a whole were notably depressed.

All the predictable features of the financial aberration were here on view. There was large leverage turning on the small interest payments by the Treasury on the public debt taken over. Individuals were dangerously captured by belief in their own financial acumen and intelligence and conveyed this error to others. There was an investment opportunity rich in imagined prospects but negligible in any calm view of the reality. Something seemingly exciting and innovative captured the public imagination, in this case the joint-stock company, although, as already noted, it was of decidedly earlier origin. (The great chartered companies trading to India and elsewhere were by now a century old.) And as the operative force, dutifully neglected, there was the mass escape from sanity by people in pursuit of profit.

Exceptional, however, was the notice this latter circumstance was eventually accorded. Charles Mackay, in a singularly acute account of the South Sea Bubble, pointed out the truth:

> [In the autumn of 1720,] public meetings were held in every considerable town of the empire, at which petitions were adopted, praying the vengeance of the legislature upon the South-Sea directors, who, by their fraudulent practices, had brought the nation to the brink of ruin. Nobody seemed to imagine that the nation itself was as culpable as the South-Sea company. Nobody blamed the credulity and avarice of the people—the degrading lust of gain...or the infatuation which had made the multitude run their heads with such frantic eagerness into the net held out for them by scheming projectors. These things were never mentioned.

Nor in the aftermath of modern speculation are they ever mentioned, as will amply be evident.

CHAPTER 5

THE AMERICAN TRADITION

The financial memory is brief, but subjective public attitudes can be more durable. As John Law created a suspicion of banks in France that endured for a century or longer, so the South Sea Bubble warned Britain against joint-stock companies. The Bubble Act restricted for many succeeding decades the formation of limited companies, what we now denote corporations. However, by 1824, these enterprises had once again gained sufficient respectability to allow another wave of London stock promotions. The latter were also inspired in part by prospects in South America, but they extended in an ecumenical way to the Red Sea. One promotion that was especially distinguished involved a company committed to the draining of that body of water "with a view to recovering the treasure abandoned by the Egyptians after the crossing of the Jews." Later in the century there were further speculative episodes in response to opportunities in the New World, with South America once again serving as a special magnet for the imagination. In 1890, the Bank of England had to pull the great house of Baring Brothers back from bankruptcy caused by its perilous involvement in Argentine loans. No one should suppose that the modern misadventures in Third World loans are at all new.

Whatever the London excesses, there can, however, be no trace of chauvinism in saying that in the last century the speculative imagination was at work in its most ardent form in the United States. This was because of a special American commitment to the seeming magic of money creation and its presumptively wondrous economic effects.

The commitment to monetary magic began in colonial times. Again, as so reliably in financial matters, those involved were persuaded of their own innovative genius; as before and as ever, they were reinventing the wheel.

The Southern colonies—Maryland, Virginia, and Carolina as it then was called—issued notes against the security of tobacco and greatly deplored any demand for gold or silver as a means of payment, on occasion proscribing their use. In Maryland, notes based on tobacco served as currency for nearly two centuries, longer by a considerable margin than the gold standard was to last. But it served prosaically as compared with the paper currency of New England.

In 1690, Sir William Phips led an expedition of markedly informal soldiers from the Massachusetts Bay Colony to the fortress of Quebec. It was intended that what they captured there would pay the costs of their foray. Alas, the fortress did not fall, and when the troops returned, there was no hard money, no gold or silver coin, in the colonial treasury to pay them. It then seemed a minor step for the colonial government to issue paper notes

Massachusetts' coffers were bare when Sir William Phips (above) and his markedly informal band of soldiers failed to capture the fortress and fortunes of Quebec.

promising eventual payment in gold or silver;
for two decades thereafter the paper circulat-
ed side by side and at par with the metals on
the basis of this promise. Here a seemingly innovative and wonderful financial instrument
and here again the special wonder of leverage.
This was debt in the form of the paper notes
backed by markedly fewer solid assets, mean-
ing hard money, than were available should
all the notes be presented at once for payment.

The wonder spread to other colonies; notes
were issued in abundance, indeed with abandon. Rhode Island was an extreme case.
There, as elsewhere, on the eventual days of
reckoning, the notes became worthless or
nearly so.

Not all the colonies, it should be said, suc-
cumbed; Pennsylvania, New York, New
Jersey, Delaware, and Maryland exercised admirable restraint. And there is indication that
the paper money, sustaining, as it did, prices
and trade, contributed to general economic
well-being where it was so used. This was certainly the view of Benjamin Franklin, who
could have been influenced by being in business himself as a printer of the notes.
Eventually, in 1751, the Parliament in

London forbade the paper issues in New England and, a little later, elsewhere in the colonies.

There was sharp anger over this action; paper and its associated leverage remained strongly in the minds of the American colonists as an economic good. Nor should the use of paper be wholly condemned, although many historians have done so. Washington's soldiers were paid in Continental notes; by these the Revolution was financed. Tax receipts were then negligible, as was the machinery for tax collection. The cost of the war was thus borne by those who, receiving the so-called Continentals, found their buying power quickly and irrevocably diminishing. Thus was American independence purchased, and it is not clear that it could have been bought in any other way. The stage was now set for recurrent speculative episodes in the new republic.

Influenced initially by the still-fresh memory of the inflation brought about by the Continental currency, the hugely available supply of paper chasing a necessarily limited supply of goods—shoes in Virginia at $5,000 a pair, more than $1,000,000 for a full outfit of clothing—the new country's financial policy was conservative. The Constitution forbade the federal government and, needless to say, also the states to issue paper money. Business would be done with gold and silver and bank notes redeemable in metal. A central bank, the First Bank of the United States, was created to enforce discipline on the small scattering of state-chartered banks by refusing to accept the notes of those that did not pay out in specie on demand. The by-now conservative Northeast approved this action; the new and financially more needful South and West most certainly did not. Easy credit from amply available bank notes was there greatly valued. In 1810, under attack for its financial rigor, the charter of the Bank was not renewed.

With the stimulus of the War of 1812 and the need to finance it by extensive public borrowing, prices rose. State banks, relieved of the burden of the forced redemption, were now chartered with abandon; every location large enough to have "a church, a tavern, or a blacksmith shop was deemed a suitable place for setting up a bank." These banks issued notes, and other, more surprising enterprises, imitating the banks, did likewise. "Even barbers and bartenders competed with the banks in this respect...." The assets back of these notes were, it need hardly be said, minuscule and evanescent. Leverage once again.

In the years following the end of the war, land and other property values throughout the country rose wonderfully; as is always the case, the rising values attracted those who were persuaded that there would be yet further increases and from this persuasion ensured that there would be yet greater increases to come. The Second Bank of the United States was chartered in 1816—the feeling that such higher regulatory authority was needed had persisted. However, initially it added to the boom; the Bank involved itself enthusiastically in real estate loans. Then, in 1819, the boom collapsed. Prices and property values fell drastically; loans were foreclosed; the number of bankruptcies went up. This was the first of the speculative episodes with resulting collapse that were to characterize American economic and financial history for the rest of the century. The word *panic* as it pertained to money entered the language. Later, in eager search of milder, less alarming reference, *crisis, depression, recession,* and now, of course, *growth adjustment* came successively to denote the economic aftermath.

It seems likely, although no one knows for sure, that the boom of the second decade of the last century came to an end in 1819 in the normal course of the speculative episode. But the Second Bank, which, in keeping with its regulatory purpose, had begun calling in the notes for payment, was intuitively and sharply blamed. As always, the need was to find a cause apart from the speculation itself. In consequence, President Andrew Jackson rallied public opinion against such institutions, an effort in which he was unintentionally aided by Nicholas Biddle of Philadelphia. As head of the Bank, Biddle called on the local country banks with elitist, righteous, and generally offensive vigor to make good on their notes. In consequence, the charter of the Second Bank, like that of the First, was not renewed. Nearly a century would pass before a central bank would again be tolerated in the United States. Soon new banks and bank notes flooded onto the scene. The stage was set for the next speculative episode, which was to end in the crash of 1837.

This speculative bubble was once again in real estate, especially in the West and including claims on the public lands, but it extended to manufacturing enterprises and commodities as well. It was financed by the borrowing of the notes proliferated by the ever-increasing number of banks. But now there was also a new source of financing.

Internal improvements, as they were called, became a major investment opportunity. These, notably canals and turnpikes, addressed the great distances and formidable landscape over which it was necessary for the products of farm, mine, and factory to travel in the new republic. The states took up the task of finding the funds; these proved to be available in volume from Britain. Money moved in unprecedented amounts across the Atlantic, and without question it contributed affirmatively to the construction of transportation facilities. But it also contributed to an explosive boom in business and employment and to a rush to share in the appreciating property values.

In 1837 came the inevitable disenchantment and collapse. A period of marked depression again ensued. This episode did, however, have two new features—one of them of continuing significance today. It clearly left behind the improvements, notably the canals, which had been the source of the speculative enthusiasm. And it introduced a distinctly modern attitude toward the loans that were outstanding: in the somber conditions following the crash, these were viewed with indignation and simply not repaid. Mississippi, Louisiana, Maryland, Pennsylvania, Indiana, and Michigan all repudiated their debts, although there was some mild later effort at repayment. Anger was expressed that foreign banks and investors should now, in hard times, ask for payment of debts so foolishly granted and incurred. A point must be repeated: only the pathological weakness of the financial memory, something that recurs so reliably in this history, or perhaps our indifference to financial history itself, allows us to believe that the modern experience of Third World debt, that now of Argentina, Brazil, Mexico, and the other Latin American countries, is in any way a new phenomenon.

For a decade after the bursting of the debt bubble in 1837, business conditions were depressed in the United States. The number of banks available for financing speculative adventures declined. Then, after another 10 years, public memory faded again. Confidence returned, bank charters exfoliated, bank notes once more became available to finance speculation, and in 1857 there was another panic and collapse.

Meanwhile there had been an experience of leverage that would have seemed formidable to T. Boone Pickens or even Michael Milken and the once-great house of Drexel Burnham Lambert. State regulation required banks to hold reserves of hard coin against their outstanding notes. This was to limit in a sensible way the length of the lever. Bank examiners enforced this requirement, but the enforcement was on a par with that recently of the regulations on the savings and loan industry. At the outer extreme of compliance, a group of Michigan banks joined to cooperate in the ownership of the same reserves. These were transferred from one institution to the next in advance of the examiner as he made his rounds. And on this or other occasions, there was further economy; the top layer of gold coins in the container was given a more impressive height by a larger layer of ten-penny nails below. But not all of the excesses of leverage were in the West. In these same years, in the more conservative precincts of New England, a bank was closed up with $500,000 in notes outstanding and a specie reserve of $86.48 in hand.

The Civil War did not alter the sequence of speculative boom and bust, but it shortened the interval between episodes. As the wounds of war healed in the late 1860s and early 1870s, there came one of the greatest of speculative booms portending the economically and politically devastating panic of 1873.

The preceding years were ones of generally increasing and pyramiding values and generally euphoric conditions in manufacturing, farming, and public construction. Increasing values again brought increasing values. As with the canals and turnpikes, it was transportation, this time the railroads, that was the focus of the speculation. Here the horizons seemed truly without limit. Who could lose on what was so obviously needed? Again, British loans became available in huge volume, these sustained by the financial amnesia

that had now erased all effective memory of
the defaulted loans of 40 years before. Soon
the reality. The new railroads, and some old

The great railroad boom of the 19th century ended
in corruption and imaginative manipulation of the
prices of railroad stocks. Above, railroad officials
celebrate the completion of the first transcontinen-
tal rail line in 1869 in Promontory, Utah.

ones, could not pay. The respected banking house of Jay Cooke & Company, heavily involved with railroad financing, failed in September of 1873. Two large banks also went under. The New York Stock Exchange was closed for 10 days. Banks in New York and elsewhere suspended payment in hard coin.

Once again, in the aftermath there was the predictable escapism. This, by now, was an American tradition. The problem was not, it was said, the earlier euphoria but something amiss with money. The alleged reason for the earlier collapses, also involving money, had been the unduly heavy hand of the two Banks of the United States; now the cause was said to be a little-noticed plan of a short time earlier to retire the Civil War greenbacks and move to a gold standard. Nothing, given the history and the fascination with paper, could appeal more reliably to the American mind. Born forthwith were two great political movements, that of the Greenback Party and that of the advocates of the free coinage of silver. And soon to come was the resonant voice of William Jennings Bryan and its warning as to the American crucifixion on the cross of gold.

In the last decades of the last century, given

the broad deflationary tendency of the time, there was a strong case for a more liberal monetary regime. Those who so urged were not wrong. But then, as ever, the effect of the monetary agitation was to divert attention from the role of the earlier speculation and its inevitable and depressive aftereffect.

The economist Joseph Schumpeter held that recurrent mania was a normal feature of business life.

From the neatly timed sequence of boom and bust in the last century came, in later years, another design to conceal the euphoric episode. That, in effect, was to normalize it. Boom and bust were said to be predictable manifestations of the business cycle. Mania there might be, as Joseph Schumpeter thus characterized it, but mania was a detail in a larger process, and the benign role of the ensuing contraction and depression was to restore normal sanity and extrude the poison, as some other scholars put it, from the system. University courses on business cycles now accepted as routine the alternation between high, even extravagant, expectations and low.

In 1907, after another, less dramatic escape from reality, this one centering on New York, there came what was called the Wall Street panic. It remains memorable for the belief that J. P. Morgan, calling on public and private funds to rescue the endangered Trust Company of America and calling also on New York clergymen to preach sermons of confidence and encouragement, single-handedly brought it to an end. This is questionable. A crash can come to an end without divine intervention.

J. P. Morgan was credited with ending the crash of 1907 by, along with other remedial action, asking the clergy of New York City to preach sermons of encouragement.

Again, in the months following World War I, there was a mildly euphoric mood. Farm income was good; from this came a speculative surge in land purchases and in farm land prices. This left farmers with a heavy burden of debt, which in the years of the Great Depression was commonly estimated to exceed in the aggregate the value of all rural property. Born here were the agricultural crisis of the 1930s and the farm programs that still exist to support farm prices and income and supply farmers with credit.

But overshadowing all previous speculative episodes was the great stock-market boom of the later 1920s. Not since John Law or the Bubble had mania seized so deeply so large and influential a sector of the population. Here on display were all the basic features of financial euphoria. Here too was an end to the Schumpeterian notion that the ensuing contraction was normal, tolerable, and, as he urged, benign.

C H A P T E R   6

1929

In the larger history of economics and finance, no year stands out as does 1929. It is,
as I have elsewhere observed—like 1066,
1776, 1914, 1945, and now, perhaps, with
the collapse of Communism, 1989—richly
evocative in the public memory. That is partly because the speculative debacle that then
occurred was of special magnitude, even
grandeur, and more because it ushered in for
the United States and the industrial world as a
whole the most extreme and enduring crisis
that capitalism had ever experienced.

Nineteen twenty-nine is also remembered
because there were then evident all the elements of the euphoric episode and especially

the powerful commitment to presumed financial innovation. This last included, as ever, the rediscovered wonders of leverage, presently to be examined, and the parade of publicly celebrated genius. Optimism built on optimism to drive prices up. Then came the crash and the eventual discovery of the severe mental and moral deficiencies of those once thought endowed with genius and their consignment, at best, to oblivion, but, more grimly, to public obloquy, jail, or suicide. In 1929 and for years thereafter, all this was larger than life.

The justifying mood was the political, social, and economic order that was associated with the benign and, inevitably, Republican administration of Calvin Coolidge and his Treasury Secretary, Andrew W. Mellon. Then, beginning on March 4, 1929, came the presidency of the more experienced engineer, administrator, and statesman Herbert Hoover. It was a mood to be repeated a little less than 60 years later with the advent of Ronald Reagan. This recurrence was not entirely an accident. Most of those who manage investment operations or who have sizable amounts of money to invest are, indeed, Republican in their politics. Naturally, perhaps inevitably, they believe in the politicians they support, the doctrines these profess, and the economic advantage flowing therefrom. It is especially easy for those seemingly so blessed to be persuaded of the new and approximately infinite opportunities for enrichment inherent in a Republican age under a Republican regime. So in 1929; so again before the crash in 1987. All so vulnerable and all so affected, whatever their politics, should be warned.

The first manifestation of the euphoric mood of the 1920s was seen not on Wall Street but in Florida—the great Florida real estate boom of the middle of that decade. Present, apart from the optimism engendered by Coolidge and Mellon, was the undoubted attraction of the Florida climate—to many, in its contrast with that of New York or Chicago, a shining discovery. And present also was leverage; lots could be purchased for a cash payment of around 10 percent. Each wave of purchases then justified itself and stimulated the next. As the speculation got fully under way in 1924 and 1925, prices could be expected to double in a matter of weeks. Who need worry about a debt that would so quickly be extinguished?

There were other compelling forces. Choice "beachfront" lots could, by a flexible approach to mensuration, be 10 or 15 miles from the water. The noted Charles Ponzi of Boston, whose name is durably associated with investment operations that paid handsome dividends to earlier investors from the money coming in from later ones, had turned now to the real estate business. He developed a subdivision said

Charles Ponzi was already a convicted forger and larcenist when he began a new career selling swampland in Florida to unduly eager investors.

to be "near Jacksonville"; it was approximately 65 miles away. The momentum continued; such was the pressure on the serving railroads that they were forced to embargo unnecessary freight, including the building materials useful for the construction boom.

In 1926 came the inevitable collapse. The supply of new buyers needed to sustain the upward thrust dried up; there was a futile rush to get out. External and not wholly implausible explanations were available. Not the built-in culminating end of speculation but two especially vicious hurricanes from the

The 1920s Florida land boom came to an end when the supply of new and adequately gullible buyers dwindled and thousands were left homeless after a hurricane.

Caribbean in the autumn of 1926 were held to be at fault. Thousands were, indeed, left homeless. The responsibility for the debacle was thus shifted from man and his capacity for financial delusion to God and the weather. Also, if slightly, to misguided charitable enterprises in response to the wind. An official of the Seaboard Air Line was quoted in *The Wall Street Journal* as expressing the fear that the solicitation of Red Cross funds for hurricane relief would "do more damage permanently to Florida than would be offset by the funds received."

In 1925, bank clearings in Miami were $1,066,528,000; in 1928, they were down to $143,364,000.

By 1928, the speculative mood and mania had shifted to the far less equable climate of lower Manhattan.

Prices of common stock on the New York Stock Exchange had begun rising in 1924. The increase continued in 1925; suffered some setback in 1926, possibly in sympathetic reaction to the collapse of the Florida land boom; rose again in 1927; and, as it may properly be said, took clear leave of reality in 1928 and particularly in 1929.

In the spring of 1929, there was a mild break. The Federal Reserve Board, departing very slightly from its then unexampled timidity and accepted incompetence, announced that it might tighten interest rates to arrest the boom, and the market receded a bit. The action of the central bank was seen as an exercise in economic sabotage. Charles E. Mitchell, head of—as it then was—the National City Bank and himself riding the up-

Charles Mitchell, head of the National City Bank in 1929, offered to lend the public enough money to off-set any unwanted restraints by the Federal Reserve.

ward wave, stepped in to counter the threat. "We feel," he said of his bank in a statement of nearly unparalleled arrogance, "that we have an obligation which is paramount to any Federal Reserve warning, or anything else, to avert any dangerous crisis in the money market." The National City Bank would lend money as necessary to offset any restraint by the Federal Reserve.

The effect was more than satisfactory: the market took off again. In the three summer months, the increase in prices outran all of the quite impressive increase that had occurred during the entire previous year.

By now the wholly predictable and more than adequately identified features of the great speculative episode were again present and evident. Prices were going up because private investors or institutions and their advisers were persuaded that they were going up more, and this persuasion then produced the increase. Leverage was magnificently available, indeed a special marvel of the time. In its most commonplace form, it allowed the purchase of stock on a 10 percent margin—10 percent from the aspiring owner, 90 percent from the obliging lender. It wasn't cheap; by that summer the borrower paid at the then incredible interest rates of from 7 to 12 percent and once as high as 15.

The closed-end investment trusts of United Founders Corporation, Goldman, Sachs, and many other similar enterprises were especially celebrated for their genius in discovering and using leverage. The United Founders group, tracing back to an original promotion in 1921, foundered and was rescued with a $500 infusion of capital from a friend. It then borrowed money and sold securities to finance investment in other securities for an eventual total of around a billion dollars. This—assets worth a billion dollars from an original investment of $500—could have been the most notable exercise of leverage of all time, those Michigan banks and the notes leveraged against the ten-penny nails possibly excepted.

As dramatic was the leveraged extravaganza sponsored by Goldman, Sachs.

The Goldman Sachs Trading Corporation was launched by Goldman, Sachs in late 1928 with the sole purpose of holding and speculating in common stocks. The first stock offering was modest—$100,000,000, which went, as noted, to buy other securities. The following summer the Trading Corporation launched the Shenandoah Corporation, selling its stock and preferred stock to the public but retaining ultimate common-stock control in its own hands. The purpose of Shenandoah, also, was to buy and hold common stock; all gains in the value of the stock so held accrued to the holders of the common stock—including, notably, the Trading Corporation—and not to those of the fixed-return preferred. Then Shenandoah launched the Blue Ridge Corporation, repeating the process. The leveraged increase in the value of the Blue Ridge common stock accrued to the common-stock holdings of Shenandoah. These values, in turn, were reflected in yet greater magnitude to the holdings of the Trading Corporation.

Unrecognized only was the way in which this process would work in reverse—the fixed obligations commanding diminishing market values and revenues of the stocks. Diminution there was. The shares of the Goldman Sachs Trading Corporation were issued at $104 and rose to $222.50 a few months later; in the late spring of 1932, they stood at $1.75.

The most celebrated men of the time were those riding and furthering the boom. Most notable were the Canadian Arthur W. Cutten; the perversely named Bernard E. "Sell 'Em Ben" Smith; the especially celebrated market operator M. J. Meehan; the two great bank chairmen, the hitherto-mentioned Mitchell of the National City and Albert H. Wiggin of the Chase; the Swedish match king and international financier extraordinary Ivar Kreuger; and Richard Whitney, the most eminent and aristocratic of brokers, and vice-president, soon to become president, of the New York Stock Exchange. Supporting them and sustaining public confidence was a convocation of economics professors who assured all listeners that what was happening was well within the norms of contemporary and successful capitalism.

Irving Fisher, a truly renowned economist at Yale, was caught up by the speculative euphoria of 1929.

The most prominent and most to be regretted of the academic sages was Irving Fisher of Yale—as already indicated, the most innovative economist of his time. Heavily involved in the market himself, he too surrendered to the basic speculative impulse, which is to believe whatever best serves the good fortune you are experiencing. In the autumn of 1929, he gained enduring fame for the widely reported conclusion that "stock prices have reached what looks like a permanently high plateau."

There was also optimistic expression from Harvard, Michigan, Ohio State, and notably from a young Princeton economist, one Joseph Stagg Lawrence, who, as stocks reached their peak, offered the widely quoted comment, "The consensus of judgment of the millions whose valuations function on that admirable market, the Stock Exchange, is that stocks are not at present overvalued." He added the question, "Where is that group of men with the all-embracing wisdom which will entitle them to veto the judgment of this intelligent multitude?"

A few did, and they did not escape articulate and even savage denunciation. As earlier noted, Paul M. Warburg, who, at least until he spoke out against the market, had been one of the most respected bankers of his time, was especially condemned, as was the equally well-known, if somewhat less reputable, Roger Babson.

Beginning on October 21 came the end.

The sequence of events that made the history of those days has often been detailed, and there is little need for an extended account here. The market opened badly the week of October 21, with heavy trading by the standards of the time. Things turned worse on Wednesday; Thursday was the first of the days of disaster. Prices dropped seemingly without limit that morning; the ticker, as had been the case on Monday, ran well behind the trading. Calls went out for more margin to people who knew not their full misfortune. The common reference was again to panic.

However, at noon on that Thursday things turned briefly for the better. The great bankers of the time, including Thomas Lamont of Morgan's, Mitchell of the National City, and Wiggin of the Chase, met at the House of Morgan and resolved to do something about it. Richard Whitney, the Morgan broker, then appeared on the floor of the Exchange to make stabilizing purchases with money the great bankers had placed at his disposal. As in the days of John Law, the Bubble, and other episodes, it was thought

The Great Crash forced stock-market innocents into selling off personal assets such as this 1929 Chrysler Roadster, which at the time had a list price of $1,555.

that by reassuring statement and action all could again be made as before. Alas, and predictably, the confidence evaporated over the weekend. There was heavy selling on Monday; Tuesday, October 29, was, until that time, the most devastating day in the history of the Exchange. Nothing now arrested the rush to sell or the likelihood of being sold out. Things were not helped by the rumor that the great bankers were themselves getting out, which may well have been the case. In succeeding weeks, Mondays being particularly bad days, the market went on down.

How little, it will perhaps be agreed, was either original or otherwise remarkable about this history. Prices driven up by the expectation that they would go up, the expectation realized by the resulting purchases. Then the inevitable reversal of these expectations because of some seemingly damaging event or development or perhaps merely because the supply of intellectually vulnerable buyers was exhausted. Whatever the reason (and it is unimportant), the absolute certainty, as earlier observed, is that this world ends not with a whimper but with a bang.

In the aftermath of the crash, there were two other predictable developments. John

Law, living out his last and dismal years in Venice, may have been more fortunate in his fate than the great financial wizards of the 1920s. Charles Mitchell and Albert Wiggin were both peremptorily sacked. Mitchell, deeply involved in the market, spent much of the next decade in court defending himself against income tax evasion charges. He had unloaded his depreciated stock on his possibly unsuspecting wife and taken a major capital-loss deduction. On the criminal charges he eventually won acquittal, but he faced heavy civil charges and payments. Wiggin, also a large operator and heavily short in the stock of his own bank, was denied his pension. Cutten, Meehan, and Sell 'Em Ben Smith were called before congressional committees. Cutten suffered from acute amnesia; Meehan, when summoned, absent-mindedly went abroad but soon came back and apologized. Richard Whitney went to Sing Sing for embezzlement. In Paris in 1932, Ivar Kreuger, once a world-class financier, promoter, and speculator and now established as a major larcenist, went out one day, bought a pistol, and shot himself. Along with much else, he had been discovered to have counterfeited Italian government bonds—an undue manifestation of the freedom of the press. Irving Fisher lost millions and was rescued in a modest way by Yale. Two giants of the time, Joseph P. Kennedy and Bernard Baruch, were to share the rewards and lasting esteem that came from having gotten out early.

Predictable also in the ensuing explanations of events was the evasion of the hard reality. This was in close parallel with what had occurred in previous episodes and was to have remarkable, sometimes fanciful, replication in 1987 and after. The market in October 1929 was said only to be reflecting external influences. During the previous summer there had been, it was belatedly discovered, a weakening in industrial production and other of the few currently available economic indices. To these the market, in its rational way, had responded. Not at fault were the speculation and its inevitable aftermath; rather, it was those deeper, wholly external influences. Professional economists were especially cooperative in advancing and defending this illusion. A few, when dealing with the history, still are.

They were not, however, completely persuasive. Some steps were taken—the creation of the Securities and Exchange Commission;

restraints on holding-company pyramiding, which had been particularly great in electric utilities; the control of margin requirements—and these were not without value. But, as ever, the attention was on the instruments of speculation. Nothing was said or done or, in fact, could be done about the decisive factor—the tendency to speculation itself.

The crash in 1929, however, did have one therapeutic effect: it, somewhat exceptionally, lingered in the financial memory. For the next quarter of a century securities markets were generally orderly and dull. Although this mood lasted longer than usual, financial history was not at an end. The commitment to Schumpeter's mania was soon to be re-asserted.

OCTOBER REDUX

Let it be emphasized once more, and especially to anyone inclined to a personally rewarding skepticism in these matters: for practical purposes, the financial memory should be assumed to last, at a maximum, no more than 20 years. This is normally the time it takes for the recollection of one disaster to be erased and for some variant on previous dementia to come forward to capture the financial mind. It is also the time generally required for a new generation to enter the scene, impressed, as had been its predecessors, with its own innovative genius. Thus impressed, it becomes bemused by the two further influences operating in this world that are greatly seductive of error. The first, as sufficiently noted, is the ease with which any individual, on becoming affluent, attributes his good fortune to his own superior acumen. And there is the companion tendency of the many who live in more modest circumstances to presume an exceptional mental aptitude in those who, however evanescently, are identified with wealth. Only in the financial world is there such an efficient design for concealing what, with the passage of time, will be revealed as self- and general delusion.

There are, however, exceptions to any rule. While the 20-year cycle from illusion to disillusion and back to illusion had a superb regularity in the United States in the last century, some of the more violent episodes of irrationality—those of John Law, the South Sea Bubble, and the crash of 1929 being examples—did remain more vividly in the financial as well as the general public memory. The result was a somewhat longer period of doubt, caution, and comparative sanity.

The crash of 1929 ushered in the dismal years of the Great Depression, for which, indeed, the stock-market debacle should rightly be held sharply responsible. In the weeks that immediately followed, demand for a wide range of consumers' goods weakened, business confidence was shaken, and, as a direct manifestation, business investment fell and business failures rose. Economists, as I have noted, then as later sought to exculpate the market, holding deeper factors, including now insufficiently relaxed Federal Reserve policy, responsible for the business decline. This was evasion bordering on nonsense. In fact, the market crash broke into an exceptionally fragile financial, banking, and general economic structure. There can be no plausible doubt that it had a substantial and ultimately devastating economic effect.

By the mid-1950s, however, Americans were ceasing to regard the stock market with the misgiving—the sense that it was somehow designed for their expropriation— that was the attitude in the aftermath of the 1929 crash. In 1954 and 1955, a quarter of a century after the terrible October days, there was a modest boom.

Later in that decade and throughout the 1960s, there were further speculative upsurges and ensuing breaks. These were years of good, frequently brilliant, performance by the

American and other industrial economies—low unemployment, steady and ample economic growth, and low rates of inflation. Reflecting the accompanying optimism, youthful market operators, notably the Go-Go boys of the 1960s, were believed by others and, as ever, by themselves to have a new

and highly innovative approach to investment opportunities. Relatively mild setbacks from time to time, principally in 1962 and 1969, at least partially corrected this error.

The most notable manifestation of the new speculative mood, while under markedly American auspices, was to occur in Switzerland, with an outreach over Europe and down into South America.

Bernard Cornfeld now lives quietly in France. He dabbles in real estate and is said to be thinking of reentering the mutual-fund business.

Investors Overseas Services (IOS) was the brainchild—some would say brainstorm—of an indubitably energetic group of young men led by Bernard Cornfeld and Edward Cowett—the first a former social worker, the second an unquestionably accomplished lawyer. IOS, in turn, was the guiding force for a large group of mutual funds; of mutual funds investing in other mutual funds (the Fund of Funds), including incestuous investment in funds of the IOS itself; and of firms to sell mutual funds and to manage mutual funds and, at a somewhat ethereal level, banks, insurance companies, and other financial entities. But, most of all, it was a vast sales organization in which securities salesmen recruited other salesmen and received a commission on their sales, and those so recruited, in turn, recruited yet other vendors and got commissions. The pyramid in Germany was eventually some six stories high, and only a fraction of the original investment found its way into the securities it was meant to buy. The rest went into all those commissions.

One would have difficulty imagining a fiscally more improbable enterprise for the investor. IOS was forbidden by the Securities and Exchange Commission to sell securities in the United States and in later times to American citizens wherever they lived. Thus its offshore designation. It was extruded from Brazil, normally considered a financially tolerant venue. It had recurrent problems with the Swiss and, in the end, was forced to move many of its operations to a closely adjacent site in France. Nonetheless, IOS extracted some billions of dollars from bemused investors, not excluding the salesmen of the firm itself, who were extensively captured by their own sales oratory. James Roosevelt, a son of F.D.R., formerly a distinguished member of Congress and an ambassador to the United Nations; Sir Eric Wyndham White, a highly regarded international civil servant and longtime secretary-general of GATT (the General Agreement on Tariffs and Trade); and Dr. Erich Mende, a former vice-chancellor of the German Federal Republic, all lent their names in evident good faith to the enterprise. They and thousands of others responded happily to the compelling Cornfeld appeal, "Do you sincerely want to be rich?"

This was to be to their eventual regret. Invited to join the board of directors by James Roosevelt, I had declined. I had a general rule against serving on corporate boards, and it had been powerfully reinforced in this case by more specific misgivings emerging from both the comments of Swiss bankers of my acquaintance and my own knowledge of the perils of such enterprises. To have so served would, one cannot doubt, have had certain adverse effects on my economic reputation.

Readers would have been spared this treatise.

In 1969, declining sales and securities prices worked their way back through the sales organization with highly leveraged reverse effect. Desperate efforts to hold up values by inside purchase failed, as was inevitable given the flooding disenchantment. Cornfeld was persuaded, it seems unfortunately, to yield the substantial remaining assets to Robert Vesco.

Robert Vesco, the fugitive financier who has been given refuge in Cuba, took control of Investors Overseas Services in 1971.

Such is the latter's financial reputation that he has wisely avoided American residence ever since. Bernard Cornfeld himself was not charged with any criminal activity, although later, in consequence, it would seem, of an unwise passage through Switzerland, he was detained for some weeks in a Swiss jail. It is difficult to believe that he was guilty of anything beyond his own misguided energy and ambition. The guilt lies, as always, with those who sought so eagerly and by such a transparent device to be so separated from their money.

In these years there were also the enthusiastic reception given the Real Estate Investment

Trusts, the REITs, and, as time passed, the self-congratulatory enthusiasm of the large international banks—Citibank, Manufacturers Hanover, Continental Illinois, and others—as they received the sizable deposits of the OPEC oil-producing countries and sent them on in the form of loans to Mexico, Brazil, Argentina, Poland, and other eager recipients. This recycling, as it was called, was considered innovative and imaginative at the time as well as an operation at the highest level of financial respectability. Its legacy, so sadly apparent since, was either default or an oppressive burden of debt for the countries so favored, a burden gravely threatening their living standards and the stability of their governments. Some, perhaps much, of the borrowed money was further recycled, without local benefit, to Switzerland or back to New York. It is not certain that the bankers responsible, protected by that high repute that goes with association with great assets, have ever themselves fully realized their error.

The more limited episodes of the 1960s and 1970s and their unhappy consequences sufficiently established that financial aberration was still the norm. The full revelation remained, however, for the 1980s, leading on to the spectacular debacle of October 19, 1987.

There was, as before, little that was new in this speculative episode. All of the elements were again and predictably in place. As the age of Calvin Coolidge had been hailed, so now the age of Ronald Reagan. Leverage came back in the form of corporate takeovers and leveraged buyouts, small ownership and control made possible by large debt. There was the requisite new financial instrument that was thought to be of stunning novelty: bonds with a high risk and thus carrying a high interest rate. Their novelty, as noted, resided only in their deeply valid name—junk bonds.

A new generation of young men on Wall Street exhibited the necessarily abbreviated memory. And there was the adulation of especially dramatic operators, who were, in fact, on their way to disgrace and prison. (Dennis Levine and Ivan Boesky, the most famed of the new generation, were so consigned before the crash.) Michael Milken and Drexel Burnham Lambert, the principal promoters of

The 1987 market bust caught a younger generation of speculators of the Reagan years. Above, Wall Streeters take in the bad news.

the substitution of junk bonds for equity, also encountered difficult days in the aftermath. Mr. Milken fell afoul of the securities-regulation laws, and Drexel Burnham, after rewarding its executives for earlier achievement, suffered a spectacular descent into bankruptcy. Here, from *Fortune*, a far from radical source, is its conclusion on the latter deviation:

Did Drexel do itself in? Or was it done in? The truth is that this was a case of suicide—and murder. So potent had the firm become that employees truly believed they could do whatever they wanted without fear of retribution. That's why they could threaten Fortune 500 corporations with takeovers and never expect political retaliation. And that's why they could leverage themselves and their clients to the hilt without preparing for the day debt would go out of fashion. Says a former officer: "You see, we thought, 'We are invulnerable.'"

If they had been intellectually sensitive and acute, neither Mr. Milken nor his corporate associates would have accepted the risk of enduring personal and public disgrace. Money once again misled.

That the crash of 1987 and its results were predictable, well in the established pattern, I can avow, for, as I have earlier noted, I ventured the relevant prediction. In early 1987, I dealt with it and the parallels with 1929 in the *Atlantic* and spoke of a "day of reckoning...when the market goes down seemingly without limit," adding reference to a truth here more than sufficiently celebrated: "Then will be rediscovered the oldest rule of Wall Street: Financial genius is before the fall."

I also suggested in the article, however, that the crash, when it came, would be less devastating in its economic effect than that of 1929. Here there had been change. A welfare system, farm-income supports in what was no longer a predominantly agricultural economy, trade-union support to wages, deposit insurance for banks (and similarly for the S&Ls), and a broad Keynesian commitment by the government to sustain economic activity— things all absent after the 1929 crash—had lent a resilience to the economy. There was, in consequence, a lessened vulnerability to serious and prolonged depression.

The aftermath of the 1987 debacle saw an especially notable exercise in evasion even by the formidable standards of the past. The first response came from a convocation of former Secretaries of the Treasury, professional public spokesmen, and chief executive officers of major corporations. They joined in sponsoring a *New York Times* advertisement attributing the crash to the deficit in the budget of the federal government. This deficit had already persisted in what was considered by fiscal conservatives an alarming magnitude for the preceding six years of the Reagan administration. But then, on that terrible October morning, realization was thought to have dawned. The financial markets suddenly became aware. Again the ability of those in high financial position to provide a cloak, in this case one extending to absurdity.

Next came a series of studies—by the New York Stock Exchange (NYSE), the SEC, and a high presidential task force. These varied from the marginally relevant to the wholly ridiculous. The one commissioned by President Reagan and chaired by Nicholas F. Brady, claimed the most attention. It did not entirely overlook the preceding speculation; five or six early pages consisting mostly of charts affirmed the previous existence of a "bull market," and the report said boldly and wisely, in a comment in an appendix study, that "eventually all things, good or bad, must come to an end, and the worldwide bull market did so with a vengeance in October 1987." Neglecting this basic truth, however, the study then emphasized superbly subordinate factors—program trading, portfolio insurance, largely unspecified specialist misbehavior. ("The performance of NYSE specialists during the October market break period varied over time and from specialist to specialist.") Also, in a breathtaking leap in logic, certain regulatory controls were said to have helped cause the collapse. That speculation and its aftermath are recurrent and inherent, unfortunate characteristics of markets extending over the centuries, went mostly unmentioned.

So also in the other studies. That of the SEC, weighing in at under five pounds, was devoted entirely to market performance and "strategies" during the crash. There was no mention of the circumstances that induced it. The report said, in sum, that program trading had substituted a computer-based technological intelligence for the human version, and the technology could spill out sell orders in a sudden and unprecedented way.

Index and option trading had, indeed, added casino effects to the market. Found innocent, however, were those individuals, speculative funds, pension funds, and other institutions that had so unwisely, in naiveté and high expectation, repaired to the casino.

Hearings on the crash were convened by Congress. Legislation on certain of the casino effects were considered, but none was passed. Perhaps some inner voice advised the legislators that these measures did not have any central relevance. The recurrent and sadly erroneous belief that effortless enrichment is an entitlement associated with what is thought to be exceptional financial perspicacity and wisdom is not something that yields to legislative remedy.

O f the history and its compelling element of surprise there is no end, nor has it any defined geographical limits. In March 1990, Japanese stocks took a large and wholly unexpected dive—major stock indices on the Tokyo market went down by nearly a quarter. (Japanese ingenuity was, however, to come into play. A leading investment house concerned with Japan reported that "there was talk of changing the accounting rules, so that an institution that loses money in stocks can keep that fact confidential.") A *Washington Post* dispatch told of what had been previously expected: "It has been a matter of received wisdom...that the Japanese stock market, manipulated by the government and big investment houses, can only go up, generating funds for the nation's export assaults overseas."

In the last months, as this is written, word has come from Canada of collapse in the highly leveraged operations of Mr. Robert Campeau. These had put the continent's greatest retail houses under the burden of crushing debt. There was question as to whether they had enough money to buy the merchandise they needed to sell. Until the day of reckoning, few asked what this far-from-distinguished Canadian real estate operator, product of what has been called a roller-coaster career, could do for, say, Bloomingdale's. A sometime observer, New York retailing consultant Howard Davidowitz, said of him in *MacLean's* magazine that "he was the guy at the head of the table who was pounding his fist and yelling, 'Do the damn deal.' No one could have stopped him." Not a distinguished qualification. *Fortune* again captured the essence: "THE BIGGEST LOONIEST DEAL EVER. HOW THE WACKY ROBERT CAMPEAU AND HIS FEE-HUNGRY

BANKERS CONCOCTED A HUGE TAKEOVER THAT
PROMPTLY WENT BUST."

The bankers in question were, it need hardly be noted, among the most reputable on the
North American continent. So were those
who backed the glittering architecture of Mr.
Donald Trump and his not greatly less extravagant adventure into aviation. A word of
sympathy should be offered Mr. Campeau
and Mr. Trump. The press and the public at
large have reacted with a certain measure of
delight to their transformation from aggres-
sively avowed geniuses (in Mr.
Trump's case, avowed not least
by himself) to objects of condemnation. This is a highly selective
attitude. Almost no mention has
been made of the deeply defective
judgment of the banks that financed these men. What in the
world were they doing? Everyone
who studies television knows
that Citibank yearns to believe
that Americans wish not only to
survive but to succeed. Mention

Canadian developer
Robert Campeau was
ousted as chairman of
his corporation after
taking his enterprises
deeply and dangerous-
ly into debt.

should also be made of their wish for banker solvency and good sense. Who, one asks,

thought it wise to back these admitted adventurers with hundreds of millions of entrusted dollars? Over the country as a whole the same question arises as to those who, in error, optimism, stupidity, and forthright, generally unimaginative larceny, led the savings and loan associations into the greatest financial scandal of all time.

CHAPTER 8

REPRISE

There are few references in life so common as that to the lessons of history. Those who know it not are doomed to repeat it. The lessons of history can, however, be disturbingly ambiguous, and perhaps especially so in economics. That is because economic life is in a process of continuous transformation, and, in consequence, what was observed by earlier scholars—Adam Smith, John Stuart Mill, Karl Marx, Alfred Marshall—is an uncertain guide to the present or the future.

However, if the controlling circumstances are the same, the lessons of history are compelling—and even inescapable. That is the case here.

At the risk of repetition—restatement of what one hopes is now evident—let the lessons be summarized. The circumstances that induce the recurrent lapses into financial dementia have not changed in any truly operative fashion since the Tulipomania of 1636-1637. Individuals and institutions are captured by the wondrous satisfaction from accruing wealth. The associated illusion of insight is protected, in turn, by the oft-noted public impression that intelligence, one's own and that of others, marches in close step with the possession of money. Out of that belief, thus instilled, then comes action—the bidding up of values, whether in land, securities, or, as recently, art. The upward movement confirms the commitment to personal and group wisdom. And so on to the moment of mass disillusion and the crash. This last, it will now be sufficiently evident, never comes gently. It is always accompanied by a desperate and largely unsuccessful effort to get out.

Inherent in this sequence are the elements by which, in a comprehensive way, it is misunderstood. Those who are involved never wish to attribute stupidity to themselves. Markets also are theologically sacrosanct. Some blame can be placed on the more spec-

tacular or felonious of the previous speculators, but not on the recently enchanted (and
now disenchanted) participants. The least important questions are the ones most emphasized: What triggered the crash? Were there
some special factors that made it so dramatic
or drastic? Who should be punished?

Accepted in reputable market orthodoxy is,
as noted, the inherent perfection of the market. The market can reflect contrived or frivo-
lous wants; it can be subject to monopoly,
imperfect competition, or errors of informa-
tion, but, apart from these, it is intrinsically
perfect. Yet clearly the speculative episode,
with increases provoking increases, is within
the market itself. And so is the culminating
crash. Such a thought being theologically un-
acceptable, it is necessary to search for external influences—in more recent times, the
downturn in the summer of 1929, the budget
deficit of the 1980s, and the "market mechanisms" that brought the crash of 1987. In the
absence of these factors, the market presumably would have remained high and gone on
up or declined gently without inflicting pain.
In such fashion, the market can be held guilt-
less as regards inherently compelled error.
There is nothing in economic life so willfully

misunderstood as the great speculative episode.

The final question that remains is what, if anything, should be done? Recurrent descent into insanity is not a wholly attractive feature of capitalism. The human cost is not negligible, nor is the economic and social effect. In the aftermath of the 1929 crash, the damage was very great, and, as noted, it contributed visibly to the depression that followed. After 1987 and still at this writing, there are the heavy residue of debt from the exercise of leverage, the claims of interest as opposed to those of productive and innovative investment, and the trauma of bankruptcy. And there are the remaining effects of the losses by individuals and pension funds to the junk bonds.

Yet beyond a better perception of the speculative tendency and process itself, there probably is not a great deal that can be done. Regulation outlawing financial incredulity or mass euphoria is not a practical possibility. If applied generally to such human condition, the result would be an impressive, perhaps oppressive, and certainly ineffective body of law.

The only remedy, in fact, is an enhanced skepticism that would resolutely associate too evident optimism with probable foolishness and that would not associate intelligence with the acquisition, the deployment, or, for that matter, the administration of large sums of money. Let the following be one of the unfailing rules by which the individual investor and, needless to say, the pension and other institutional-fund manager are guided: there is the possibility, even the likelihood, of self-approving and extravagantly error-prone behavior on the part of those closely associated with money. Let that also be the continuing lesson of this essay.

A further rule is that when a mood of excitement pervades a market or surrounds an investment prospect, when there is a claim of unique opportunity based on special foresight, all sensible people should circle the wagons; it is the time for caution. Perhaps, indeed, there is opportunity. Maybe there is that treasure on the floor of the Red Sea. A rich history provides proof, however, that, as often or more often, there is only delusion and self-delusion.

N o one concluding an essay such as this can expect to escape the questions: When will come the next great speculative episode, and in what venue will it recur—real estate, securities markets, art, antique automobiles? To these there are no answers; no one knows, and anyone who presumes to answer does not know he doesn't know. But one thing is certain: there will be another of these episodes and yet more beyond. Fools, as it has long been said, are indeed separated, soon or eventually, from their money. So, alas, are those who, responding to a general mood of optimism, are captured by a sense of their own financial acumen. Thus it has been for centuries; thus in the long future it will also be.

N O T E S   O N
S O U R C E S

CHAPTER 1

The phrase about American prosperity on page 7 is quoted by Alexander Dana Noyes in *The Market Place* (Boston: Little, Brown & Company, 1938), p. 324.

The Hornblower and Weeks statement on page 8 was quoted in *The Wall Street Journal*, September 6, 1929.

CHAPTER 3

The Braudel source on pages 26–27 is *Civilization and Capitalism, 15–18th Century*, vol. II: *The Wheels of Commerce*, Sian Reynolds, trans. (New York: Harper & Row, 1982), pp. 100–101.

The quotation on page 30 is from N. W. Posthumus, "The Tulip Mania in Holland in the Years 1636 and 1637," *Journal of Economic and Business History*, vol. I, 1928–1929. It is quoted in Braudel, p. 101.

The story about the sailor on page 30 can be found in Charles Mackay's *Extraordinary Popular Delusions and the Madness of Crowds* (Boston: L. C. Page, 1932), p. 92. The first edition of this book was published in London in 1841. While superseded in some matters by later research and writing, it remains to this day one of the most engaging and colorful accounts of speculative aberration. The quotations on pages 31–32 are also from Mackay, pp. 93–95.

John Law's early life (briefly mentioned on pages 35–36) is detailed in *The Life of John Law* by H. Montgomery Hyde (Amsterdam: Home & Van Thal, 1948). See also *John Law* by Robert Minton (New York: Association Press, 1975). I have earlier dealt with Law in *Money: Whence It Came, Where It Went* (Boston: Houghton Mifflin Company, 1975).

The description of the end of John Law's life on page 41 is from Duc de Saint-Simon, *Historical Memoirs,* Lucy Norton, ed. and trans. (London: Hamish Hamilton, 1972), vol. III, p. 299; and that of the French economy on page 42 is from the same source, p. 269.

CHAPTER 4
The comment on Sir Isaac Newton's financial loss on page 44 is from Robert Wernick, "When the Bubble burst, all of England wound up broke," *Smithsonian* magazine, December 1989, p. 158.

The territorial limits of the South Sea Company that are given on page 45 are from John Carswell, *The South Sea Bubble* (Stanford, California: Stanford University Press, 1960), p. 54. This is a basic book on the Bubble.

The Mackay quotation on page 52 is from *Extraordinary Popular Delusions and the Madness of Crowds*, p. 72.

CHAPTER 5
The quotation on page 54 is from Andreas Andréadès, *History of the Bank of England*: 1640 to 1903, 2nd ed. (London: P. S. King & Son, 1924), p. 250, citing Juglar, *Les crises economiques,* p. 334.

I have dealt with the inflation described on pages 57–58 in brief form in *Money: Whence It Came, Where It Went,* pp. 58 *et seq.*

The quotation on page 58 is from Norman Angell, *The Story of Money* (New York: Frederick A. Stokes Co., 1929), p. 279, and that on page 59 is from A. Barton Hepburn, *A History of Currency in the United States*

(New York: Macmillan Publishing Company, 1915), p. 102.

The characterization "mania" on page 67 is from Joseph Schumpeter, *Business Cycles* (New York: McGraw-Hill Book Company, 1939). See especially pp. 250 *et seq.*

CHAPTER 6
The distinctive personality of the year 1929 alluded to on pages 70–71 is dealt with on the initial pages of my book *The Great Crash, 1929.* There have been several editions; the quotation from *The Wall Street Journal* on pages 74–75, the statement by Irving Fisher on page 80, and the comments by Joseph Stagg Lawrence on the same page all appear in the one published in 1988.

The statistics on bank clearings in Miami on page 75 are from Frederick Lewis Allen, *Only Yesterday* (New York: Harper & Brothers, 1931), p. 282.

CHAPTER 7
The Cornfeld question on page 92 became the title of an excellent book on Investors Overseas Services by Charles Raw, Bruce Page, and Godfrey Hodgson (New York: Viking Press, 1971).

The quotation from *Fortune* on page 97 is from the issue of May 21, 1990.

My article mentioned on pages 97–98 appeared in the January 1987 issue of the *Atlantic.*

The quotations on pages 99–100 are from the *Report of the Presidential Task Force on Market Mechanisms,* January 1988, Study I, pp. i–ii and p. 49.

The SEC study mentioned on page 100 is entitled *The October 1987 Market Break: A Report,* and it was issued by the Division of Market Regulation, U.S. Securities and Exchange Commission, in February 1988.

The comment by Howard Davidowitz on page 102 appeared in *MacLean's,* January 29, 1990, p. 48.